The PRAYER LIFE *of* JESUS

LEARNING TO PRAY LIKE THE MASTER

HAROLD VAUGHAN

Christ *Life*
PUBLICATIONS

P.O. Box 399
Vinton, VA 24179

"THE PRAYER LIFE OF JESUS"

ISBN: 0-942889-00-2
Printed in the United States of America
Copyright © 1987, 2007 by Christ Life Publications
Second Printing

Christ Life Publications
P.O. Box 399
Vinton, VA 24179
www.christlifemin.org

Cover image of Gesthemane by Alex Slobodkin / istockphoto.com

Cover design by Chris Hartzler / hartzlerhaus.com

TABLE OF CONTENTS

INTRODUCTION

Of a certainty, "Never man spake like this man" (John 7:46). Equally certain, never a man prayed like this man. The prayer life of Jesus is one of His most outstanding features.

James Stewart said, "Prayer was not only an important part in the life of Jesus, it was His life—the very breath of His being." Christ's prayer life was far richer than a mere list of requests or preferences. His prayers were much deeper than the reading of a shopping list to His heavenly Father.

In this little volume you will find gleanings from Jesus' prayer ministry presented in a devotional style. Our Lord's example will challenge every believer in his own prayer life.

May this volume be used of the Holy Spirit, along with other means, to stimulate every reader to become a praying person.

—Harold Vaughan

Chapter 1
PREEMINENCE

Now when all the people were baptized, it came to pass,
that Jesus also being baptized, and praying.
—*Luke 3:21*

Can you recall your thoughts at the time of your baptism?
Scripture tells us Jesus was *praying* when He was baptized.
Baptism for Jesus was a crisis hour. It foreshadowed His
coming death, burial, and resurrection. When Christ went
beneath the water, that "water grave" spoke of the tomb
that His body would soon be laid in. Baptism was nothing
less than a prophecy of His impending death. Yet, in the
midst of this crisis, Jesus was "baptized, and *praying*." For
us baptism is a picture of our death–union with Christ. It
shows how we have died to our old life and been resurrected

to new life. The gospel is foreshadowed here—a sacrificial death, a temporary burial, and then a physical resurrection! In the midst of this prophecy, Jesus was praying.

I believe one of the chief characteristics of Jesus is that He was a praying man. Preeminently and supremely, Jesus Christ was a praying man. The Lord Jesus was baptized in prayer before He was baptized in water. He was immersed in communion with God long before He was immersed in the Jordan river. His life was saturated in prayer.

Immediately following His immersion, the heavens opened and Jesus was anointed with the Holy Spirit to begin His earthly ministry. "Open heavens" and the Spirit's anointing are always on the heels of prayer. Often in the Christian experience the heavens seem as brass, walled over. Pointed prayer is the means of breaking through.

There is much that could be said of Jesus. In fact, the whole world could not contain the books if everything that could be said had been written about Him. But before every other thing, behind every other thing, and above every other thing, Jesus was first and foremost a praying man.

Jesus preached great messages, but He prayed first. Jesus healed the multitudes, but He prayed first. Jesus cast out demons, but He prayed first. Jesus did the Father's will and died on the cross, but He prayed, sweating blood in Gethsemane, first.

Prayer was the natural atmosphere of Christ. He lived in an environment, a climate, an aura of prayer. When astronauts go into outer space, they must take earth's atmosphere with them. If a human went into space without oxygen, he would die.

Similarly, a fish cannot survive out of water. One winter I went fishing with a good friend, and, for a change, we had good luck. We landed several fish that weighed twelve to fourteen pounds apiece. At first, they thrashed madly about. But in a matter of minutes the thrashing was reduced to a twitching of the tale, which soon gave way to stillness. That stillness soon yielded to death. Why? Because fish cannot survive out of their element.

Take a human being out of earth's atmosphere and he will die. Take a fish out of water and it will die. And if you take prayer out of a Christian's life, for all practical purposes, he will die. What's the first thing to go when a man gets away from God? Is it church attendance? No. Tithing? No. The first thing he abandons is prayer. The external activities may disappear in time but first he stops praying—he leaves his "first love." What's the first thing to return when a man meets God afresh? Is it not his prayer life?

You can't get around prayer. You can't get above prayer. And you can't go too far in prayer. Some complain of others going too far—too deep—in prayer. Our problem is not going too far; most likely, we have not gone far enough!

Prayer is not words we say; prayer is what we are. The psalmist declared, "I *give myself unto* prayer" (Psalm 109:4). The italicized words *"give myself unto"* were added to complete the sentence, but they were not in the original language. The verse could be read, "But I prayer," or "I am prayer." Robert Murray McCheyne said, "What a man is alone with God, that is what he is. Nothing more, nothing less." Prayer is soul speech. It is those heart breathings which issue from deep within.

If the church is going to go forward in our day, she must go forward on her knees. For decades some have busied themselves trying to call America back to God, but

God has been calling His people back to prayer!

"My house shall be called the house of prayer" (Matthew 21:13). Jesus' central definition of the church—a house of prayer. Churches should be cathedrals of prayer and praise. But how many churches do you know of that could be honestly described as houses of prayer? The church today is basically a preaching point and an activity generator. Prayer, if given place at all, is generally given second place. The thing Jesus was most concerned about, we tend to be the least concerned about.

"My house. . . the house of prayer," was taken from the Old Testament book of Isaiah. It expressed God's desire for His temple. Today, as believers, our bodies are the temple of the Holy Spirit. We are the dwelling place of God. "Ye also are builded together for an habitation of God through the Spirit" (Ephesians 2:22). God lives in us—our hearts are Christ's home. Man is the dwelling place of God. Paul prayed, "That Christ may dwell in your hearts" (Ephesians 3:17), or as Wuest put it, "may Christ settle down (feel at home) in your hearts." Our bodies are the tabernacles (houses) of God. And God's house is to be a house of prayer.

THE PRAYER LIFE OF JESUS

Christ was baptized in prayer.

He lived in prayer.

He even died in prayer.

Jesus was preeminently a praying man.

Chapter 2
PRACTICE

But so much the more went there a fame abroad of him:
and great multitudes came together to hear,
and to be healed by him of their infirmities.
And he withdrew himself into
the wilderness, and prayed.
—Luke 5:15-16

As great crowds came to Jesus for healing, He withdrew into the wilderness for prayer. He had plenty of work to do. Constantly He was subjected to the relentless pressure of ministry: preaching, teaching, healing, and casting out demons. Jesus prayed before His great conflict with the ecclesiastical authorities (Luke 5:16). He prayed before He taught His disciples how to pray (Luke 11:1). Our Lord routinely turned aside to pray in the middle of an incredibly busy life.

Jesus' example clearly illustrates that prayer must take priority over service, for only service that grows out of prayer demonstrates the power of the Holy Spirit. Most of us have loads of work that must be done. S.D. Gordon said, "There is more that can be done after you have prayed, but until you do pray, there is nothing you can do but pray."

Let's just pretend for a moment. Suppose you get up tomorrow morning and open your Bible for devotions. But much to your surprise, you discover all the references to prayer and the Holy Spirit have been removed, leaving lots of empty spaces. Here's the question we must all face: What difference would it make in my life if there were no such thing as prayer? What if there were no Holy Spirit? Would your lifestyle be affected? How would your heart, your home, and your church be affected? In some cases, it would make little or no difference, for much of the activity is being carried on in the energy of the flesh. The Christian life and ministry is dependent on the inner work of "Christ in you." Through the practice of prayer we exercise dependence and faith, releasing God to do what He would not do otherwise. Prayer is our declaration of dependence upon God.

Prayer Based on Relationship

Jesus prayed because of His relationship with the Father, and all who are rightly related to God will pray. As an evangelist, my family and I have traveled together from one meeting to the next in a travel trailer. Years ago my wife and I were lying in bed late one night. In those days I often stayed up late. This particular night was extremely dark—no moon light, no street light—total darkness. Suddenly, a profound thought came into my mind. Since "profound thoughts" are so rare in my case, I thought I should share it with my wife. In the blinding darkness I nudged my wife and said, "Do you know how you can know I believe you exist?" No response. Next I said, "Honey, do you know how you can know I believe you are there?" Still no answer. Then I asked, "Honey, do you know how you can know I love you?" She finally responded to my third question. Then I said, "Honey, I believe you are there and I love you. And the proof is that I am talking with you!" Because I love my wife and family I communicate with them. We converse because we have a personal relationship. It would be foolish for me to claim that I love my wife if I never spoke with her.

In like manner, if a man really believes God is there, he will pray. How on earth could a man claim to know and love God without ever talking to Him? John Bunyan said, "If thou art not a praying man, thou art not even a Christian." Many in the church today are practical atheists. They say they believe in God but virtually never pray, at least until an emergency causes them to cry out for help. This kind of prayer is not birthed in faith but in desperation. How is this better than the devils who "also believe, and tremble" (James 2:19).

Of course there are multitudes of unsaved people who pray. They pray to Allah, Mary, saints, ancestors, and to their conception of "god." Still a praying heart is an undeniable evidence of grace. God has children who may not be on speaking terms with Him, but He has no children who never communicate with Him.

Place and Posture

If you study Jesus' practice of prayer, you will find He liked to pray in a garden, up a mountain, out in the desert, and even in the wilderness. Evidently He desired the quiet place for private prayer. In fact, He admonished His disciples to pray in their "closet," secretly (Matthew 6:6).

Jesus did not pray in order to be seen of men, though He often prayed with others near Him. The "closet" or "inner chamber" can be anywhere: an open field, an automobile, a basement, or a motel room.

If you study the physical posture of Christ as He prayed, you will find sometimes He prayed while standing, such as at the tomb of Lazarus (John 11:41) or at the feeding of the five thousand (Matthew 14:19). At other times He prayed while kneeling, as He did in Gethsemane (Luke 22:41). On occasion He fell on His face and prayed (Matthew 26:39).

From this we must notice that physical posture is always secondary to our heart posture. It's not the position of our bodies that count as much as the condition of our hearts. Before we ever speak a word to the Lord, He views our hearts. It is good to kneel in prayer. But if our hearts are dirty, bent knees will not arrest the attention of God! Prayer can be made from any physical posture when the condition of the heart is right.

Persistence and Power

Notice our Lord's persistence in Luke 6:12, "And it came to pass in those days, that he went out into a mountain to pray, and continued all night in prayer to God." Here, prior to selecting the twelve apostles, Jesus invested the entire night in prayer. We too would do well to earnestly and persistently pray before selecting leaders for our churches or making decisions in our lives. After Jesus' night of prayer, the multitudes again came, "unclean spirits" were cast out, and Jesus "healed them all." So profound was His influence that day that "the whole multitude sought to touch him." Jesus' persistence in prayer did not render Him useless; rather it refreshed His spirit and renewed His strength.

"But they that wait upon the Lord shall renew their strength; they shall mount up with wings as eagles; they shall run, and not be weary; and they shall walk, and not faint" (Isaiah 40:31).

Every great achievement in the life of Jesus was preceded by prayer. Jesus prayed, and thousands were fed (Matthew 15:36, John 6:11). Jesus prayed, and Lazarus was resurrected from the dead (John 11:41-42). Jesus prayed, and He walked on the water (Matthew 14:25). Jesus never performed a miracle, spoke a great message, cast out a devil, or healed a sick body without praying first. Every extraordinary accomplishment of Jesus was born in prayer!

Even more instructive is the fact that Christ followed each great achievement with prayer. He did not linger to bask in the glory from the crowds. I believe, He sought the solitude of prayer to thank the Father for showing Himself strong on His behalf.

Prayer in Public

The recorded public prayers of Jesus are brief and to the point. Jesus openly thanked God for food and blessed it before distributing it to others (Matthew 14:19; 26:26). We too should never hesitate to bow our heads to thank God for His provision. Public prayer in a restaurant is not for show; it is to honor God by recognizing His supply. Jesus prayed aloud before the raising of Lazarus specifically so the crowds would hear (John 11: 41-42). Are you willing to pray in public, or are you ashamed to acknowledge that you know Him?

Jesus addressed His Father in public many times as in Matthew 11:25. But in each case the brevity of His public prayers suggests that His private prayers were thorough and lengthy. Private prayer prepares us for public prayer. We need to be "prayed up" in private so we need not "catch up" when called upon for public prayer.

Prayer for People

Our Lord prayed for those who despised, forsook, and abused Him (Luke 23:34). Jesus also prayed for believers (John 17:20). John tells us Jesus prayed to the Father and asked that the Comforter be given to His followers (John 14:16). Jesus often prayed for believers by name. "Simon . . . Satan hath desired to have you . . . But I have prayed for thee" (Luke 22:31-32). In Matthew 19 we also find Jesus praying for little children. And we have the assurance that Jesus is praying for us today, "seeing he ever liveth to make intercession" for us (Hebrews 7:25).

Long Prayers

At times our Lord spent long periods in prayer. The phrases "all night" (Luke 6:12) and "rising up a great while before day" (Mark 1:35) indicate the massive amounts of time Christ spent in communion with His Father.

The longest recorded prayer of Jesus is found in John 17. This entire chapter records His concluding desires for the disciples and those who would believe on Him. Through prayer like this we glean insight in the heart of Christ. The things closest to us are unveiled as we open our souls in prayer before God. If the sinless Son of God found extended seasons of prayer important, how much more do we need the benefits of quantitative time alone with God? How quickly our puny resources are exhausted unless constantly replenished in the inner chamber. Our work becomes mechanical, our witness ineffective, our word powerless, unless performed in the atmosphere of prayer.

A.T. Pierson said, "He who rushes in the Presence of God to hasten through a few formal petitions, and then hasten back to outside cares and pursuits, does not tarry long enough to lose the impression of what is without, and get the impress of what is within, the secret chamber." In order to shake off the influence of the world, we must linger sufficiently inside the veil.

Short Prayers

"My God, my God, why hast thou forsaken me?" (Matthew 27:46). Even as He suffered the torments of the Cross, Jesus prayed. On Calvary Christ took the full brunt of the judgment of God against sin. God's wrath against all sin of all time was unleashed upon His Son. Then as God turned His back on the Son, Jesus could no longer pray, "My Father." Now he was forced to pray, "My God, my God."

15

For the first time in all eternity the Son was separated from the Father. Never had He prayed like this before, and never will He pray like that again. Notice carefully that even in the depths of immeasurable torment, Jesus still prayed!

His cries on Calvary were short, pungent, and ejaculatory. He prayed, "Father, forgive them" (Luke 23:34). Jesus prayed this short but deeply spiritual prayer while the cruel mob mocked Him, and soldiers gambled for His clothes, and the disciples forsook Him. No trace of apology, no hint of guilt was expressed by the wicked soldiers who hung Him on the tree. Amazingly, our Lord prayed for those at the foot of the Cross to be forgiven their crime.

While on the cross He also prayed the three greatest words ever uttered: "It is finished." This was not primarily an announcement to the onlooking crowd. They did not understand what was taking place. This was prayer, a declaration of the highest order. The work of redemption was complete. Sensing in His spirit the ultimate climax had been reached, boldly His heart burst out the proclamation, "It is finished." In other words, "The work You gave me to do is done!"

PRACTICE

It has been said, "Prayer is the first thing wherein a righteous life begins, and the last thing where it doth end." Jesus' consistency followed through to the end. The last breath He uttered was a short prayer, "Into thy hand I commit my spirit." Immediately following this last prayer, He "gave up the Ghost" and died. Christ began His ministry in prayer, prayed all the way to Gethsemane, and even in death Jesus prayed. The prayers from the Cross offer proof that Jesus was unfailingly a Man of prayer.

So why is it that scores of professing Christians seldom pray? Why is it that many so-called Bible-believing churches have no prayer meeting? The answer is simple: we believe we can accomplish our goals in our own strength. We don't need God! Thus, prayerlessness is the highest form of pride and self-sufficiency. But Jesus said, "Without me ye can do nothing" (John 15:5). Our ability to bear spiritual fruit depends entirely on the work of Christ in our lives, and that work is born and matured in prayer. Nothing of eternal value was ever accomplished in the absence of it. Charles Wesley said, "God will do nothing apart from prayer." Whether we realize it or not, we desperately need God to energize us with His Spirit. And this anointing is the result of time alone with God.

Prayer was an integral part of the life of Christ. May we learn from Him the practice of prayer.

Andrew Bonar wrote the following in his diary on October 7, 1860, "I see that unless I keep up short prayer every day throughout the whole day, at intervals, I lose the spirit of prayer. I would never lose sight any hour of the Lamb in the midst of the throne, and if I have this sight I shall be able to pray."

Chapter 3
AFFIRMATION

And lo a voice from heaven, saying,
This is my beloved Son, in whom I am well pleased.
—Matthew 3:17

On three occasions God gave public, verbal approval to His Son. Interestingly, each of these affirmations occurred while Jesus was praying, or immediately afterward.

Approval

The first occurrence was at Jesus' baptism.

"Now . . . it came to pass that Jesus also being baptized, and praying, the heaven was opened, And the Holy Ghost descended . . . and a voice came from heaven, which said, Thou are my beloved Son; in thee I am well pleased" (Luke 3:21-22).

19

Similar words are recorded in Matthew 3:13-17, Mark 1:9-11, and John 1:29-34, but only Luke tells us that Christ was praying at His baptism.

Jesus' public ministry was about to begin. At the outset of His earthly service, a statement of His Father's satisfaction and approval was publicly declared. Christ alone could know its profound significance, but how fitting it was that the Father spoke as He was praying. At that moment the Father said, "Thou art My beloved Son: in Thee I am well-pleased."

As far as we can tell, Jesus had not yet performed a miracle, preached a sermon, or cast out one demon. Yet the Father said that He was extremely pleased with Christ. Jesus was right on track, faithfully following the Father's dictates. No doubt the Father's encouragement strengthened Jesus and encouraged Him to press on.

Glorification

Later in His ministry, Jesus gave the disciples an advance warning of His imminent death. "Except a corn of wheat fall into the ground and die, it abideth alone: but if it die, it bringeth forth much fruit" (John 12:24).

The disciples had just told Jesus about certain Greeks

who came desiring to see Him. Hearing about these inquiring Gentiles, Jesus sensed that the time of His glorification was near. He explained that the Son of Man, like a kernel of grain when it is planted, must die before He could bear much fruit. The fruit Christ was to bear would come from many nations, including both Jews and Gentiles.

Then He said, "Now is my soul troubled" (v. 27). And, as in other cases when the pressures increased, Jesus began to pray. Turning the focus from His own impending suffering, Jesus said, "Father, glorify Thy name" (v. 28a) In this prayer, He revealed the ultimate purpose of life: glorifying God. Immediately following His prayer, a voice came from heaven: "I have both glorified it, and will glorify it again" (v. 28b). God would receive the glory from Christ's redemptive work. Multitudes of rebellious sinners would be reclaimed—they would honor God and glorify His name. This is fruit indeed.

God speaks in answer to prayer. In response to Jesus' prayer, the Father purposefully spoke His confirming word in the ears of Christ's disciples. "This voice came not because of me, but for your sakes," Jesus told the bystanders

(v. 30). On this occasion, God's voice was a revelation to Jesus' followers. They were still in the dark, but soon all things would come into focus, and God's prophetic voice would be remembered.

Transformation

The Father's final statement of affirmation to His Son comes in Luke 9, where we read, "And as he prayed, the fashion of his countenance was altered, and his raiment was white and glistering" (Luke 9:29). Peter, John, and James had accompanied Jesus to the mountain to pray. The tired disciples fell asleep and were awakened with a start. Moses and Elijah were there—speaking with Jesus! But Jesus was different: He had peeled back the flesh, and the disciples saw His glory. He was transformed.

In the midst of their amazement, a cloud began to overshadow them. "And they feared as they entered into the cloud. And there came a voice out of the cloud, saying, 'This is my beloved Son: hear him.' And when the voice was past, Jesus was found alone" (Luke 9:34-36).

This terrifying experience left them dumbfounded. Even Peter was silent about it! God had spoken, and they had heard. No doubt those words, "hear Him," would linger in their minds. The Father's witness of the Son was yet another confirmation of Christ's identity.

All three times the Father's affirming voice was heard, Jesus had been praying. God clearly responded to His Son's prayers. Surely God longs to respond to our prayers as well. Praying people discern the voice of God. And prayer is the means to open our ears to discern His will.

Chapter 4
GRATITUDE

At that time Jesus answered and said, I thank thee,
O Father, Lord of heaven and earth.
—Matthew 11:25

Every good gift and every perfect gift is from above,
and cometh down from the Father.
—James 1:17a

An attitude of gratitude is essential to true spirituality. Jesus verbally thanked the Father. He provides us with an example and a lesson. And Scripture gives the command, "In every thing give thanks: for this is the will of God" (1 Thessalonians 5:18).

The Fishes

"And he took the seven loaves and the fishes, and gave

25

thanks" (Matthew 15:36). Recognizing the source of our food, our Lord openly expressed His gratefulness. Four thousand men were nourished from seven loaves and a few fishes. The miracle of multiplied bread was born out of thanksgiving.

A friend once related how one Christmas he had taken food baskets to some families who were in need. He knocked on a certain door, introduced himself, and revealed why he was there. The woman he faced, seeing the basket of food, responded abruptly, "What took you so long?" Her gross lack of appreciation was appalling. Imagine the emotions that benevolent fellow must have experienced.

Have you ever gone out of your way to bestow an act of kindness on someone and not received so much as a "thank you"? Imagine how God must feel when He pours out grace, day after day, only to have the world spit in His face through ingratitude.

Suppose you are invited to dinner at a friend's house. Upon arrival you discover your favorite meal has been prepared, and you spend an enjoyable evening together. You would not think of leaving without saying "thank you" to the host and hostess. Anyone with any manners would express appreciation for such hospitality. Yet how often we who live in God's universe partake of His daily benefits while seldom saying "thank you."

The "Cup"

"And he took the cup, and gave thanks, and gave it to them, saying, . . . this is my blood . . . which is shed for many for the remission of sins" (Matthew 26:27-28).

The cup represented Christ's blood that was to be shed, and the bread represented His body that was to be broken. How profound it is that Jesus thanked God for His own suffering and death in advance! We see in Jesus Christ One who knew His mission and graciously accepted it as from God. The writer of Hebrews exhorts us, "Looking unto Jesus . . . who for the joy that was set before him endured the cross." His divine perspective of future joy enabled Him to endure the Cross.

Nothing happens to the Spirit-led Christian except that which is filtered through the will of God. Our "cup," no matter how tragic it seems, can be welcomed as an opportunity for growth in grace. It is possible to give thanks in all things. We do not give thanks because everything is good; we give thanks because God is good. "And we know that all things work together for good to them that love God, to them who are the called according to his purpose" (Romans 8:28). Thanksgiving will be an integral part of a meaningful prayer life.

The church is made up of redeemed people called out to express gratitude to God. "Giving thanks always for all things unto God and the Father in the name of our Lord Jesus Christ" (Ephesians 5:20). The phrases "always" and "for all things" cover everything in life—the good, the not-so-good, and even the bad. All things are allowed by God and work His purpose. Jesus was able to thank the Lord for His own death prior to the event. Should not we also give thanks to God even in the difficult times of life?

The Grave

We see Jesus giving thanks at the tomb of Lazarus. Lazarus had been dead four days. At Jesus' request, "they took away the stone from the place where the dead was laid. And Jesus lifted up his eyes, and said, Father, I thank thee that thou hast heard me. And I knew that thou hearest me always" (John 11:41-42).

Jesus had been in prayer. At the tomb entrance Jesus thanked the Father for having heard Him. Our Lord was ever in communion with God the Father. There was never a need to catch up. Jesus' prayer life bulged with thanksgiving.

After prayer, "when he thus had spoken, he cried with a loud voice, Lazarus, come forth" (v. 43). Bold faith and thankfulness go hand in hand. The Lord Jesus speaks, and it is done. People who thank God have no problem believing God. Reflecting on God's benefits through thanksgiving will move an individual from a mentality of defeat to a stance of faith.

The children of Israel were forever grumbling and complaining. How often they would forget some great miracle. The parting of the Red Sea, the provision of manna in the wilderness, the miraculous plagues in Egypt—how could they have been so quick to forget? The answer is simple: they spent their time murmuring about what God had not done instead of reflecting on what God had done. The poison of ingratitude in their hearts caused little praise to be on their lips. Murmuring and unbelief go hand in hand, as thanksgiving goes with faith. Show me a complainer, and I will show you an unbelieving soul. Show me a grateful person, and I will show you a person who can believe God for things. Most of us have no problem believing our doctrinal statements, but how many of us believe God to actually work on our behalf? Thanking God builds our faith and gives us a disposition to trust God.

Let me exhort you to practically implement this vital aspect of prayer: thanksgiving. Why not take the next three days and conduct an experiment in your regular prayer time? For the next three days do not ask God for anything. Instead of asking for things, thank God for His benefits and for every thing that He brings to mind. Count your blessings. If you need something, just thank God for it in advance. Direct your prayers to God in uninterrupted thanksgiving, and see how three days of expressed gratitude will alter your entire perspective.

Chapter 5
REJOICING

In that hour Jesus rejoiced in spirit, and said, I thank thee,
O Father, Lord of heaven and earth.
—Luke 10:21a

The Seventy had just returned from a fruitful mission. Jesus had sent them out two-by-two and had given them great power. Upon their return, the joyful disciples related, "even the devils are subject unto us through thy name . . . In that hour Jesus rejoiced in spirit, and said, I thank thee, O Father" (Luke 10:17-21). Jesus rejoiced and gave thanks for the revelation of God to and through humble men.

Many conceive of Jesus exclusively as "a man of sorrows, and acquainted with grief" (Isaiah 53:3). Certainly this was true of Jesus at various times. But this was only one feature of His multi-faceted personality. At other times He showed a great capacity to rejoice in God. "God . . . hath anointed thee with the oil of gladness above thy fellows" (Hebrews 1:9). Christ knew springs of inner joy that others had never tasted. Galatians 5:22 tells us that joy is a fruit of the Holy Spirit. Anointed and filled with the Holy Spirit, Jesus' heart bubbled over with rejoicing.

Do you enjoy prayer—or endure prayer? Not every Christian has "been happy all the day" ever since he saw the light! Many believers never experience the sheer pleasure of knowing God. One of the catechisms expresses it well, "The chief end of man is to know God and enjoy Him forever." The early Christians had such enthusiasm for Christ that they were accused of being drunk! When was the last time anyone accused you of being drunk on your Christianity? George Muller, who had over 20,000 recorded answers to prayer, wrote the following in his diary on May 9, 1941.

It has pleased the Lord to teach me a truth, the benefit of which I have not lost for more than fourteen years. The point is this: I saw more clearly than ever that the first great and primary business to which I ought to attend every day was to have my soul happy in the Lord. The first thing to be concerned about was not how much I might serve the Lord, or how I might glorify the Lord, but how I might get my soul into a happy state, and how my inner man might be nourished.

I saw that the most important thing I had to do was to give myself to the reading of the Word of God—not prayer, but the Word of God. And here again, not the simple reading of the Word of God so that it only passes through my mind just as water runs through a pipe, but considering what I read, pondering over it, and applying it to my heart. To meditate on it, that thus my heart might be comforted, encouraged, warned, reproved, instructed. And that thus, by means of the Word of God, whilst meditating on it, my heart be brought into experimental communion with the Lord.

I began therefore to meditate on the New Testament from the beginning early in the morning. The first thing I did, after having asked in a few words the Lord's blessing upon His precious Word, was to begin to meditate on the Word of God, searching as it were into every verse to get blessing out of it.

When we pray, we speak to God. Now prayer, in order to be continued for any length of time in any other than a formal manner, requires, generally speaking, a measure of strength or godly desire; and the season, therefore, when this exercise of the soul can be most effectively performed is after the inner man has been nourished by meditation on the Word of God, where we find our Father speaking to us, to encourage us, to comfort us, to instruct us, to humble us, to reprove us.

By the blessing of God, I ascribe to this mode the help and strength which I have had from God to pass in peace through deeper trials, in various ways, than I had ever had before.

How different, when the soul is refreshed and made happy early in the morning, from what it is when, without spiritual preparation, the service, the trials, and the temptations of the day come upon me!

George Mueller had learned how to rejoice in God

through intentional, personal fellowship with Him every day. By means of Word-centered fellowship with God, Mr. Mueller learned to put his soul "into a happy state" before God.

Divine Contact

What thrilled the heart of Jesus? What caused Him to be joyful? The psalmist says, "in thy presence is fulness of joy" (Psalm 16:11). God's personal presence is the source of true joy. Jesus knew the abiding presence of His Father.

The sheer thrill of being on speaking terms with the Father brought deep joy to Jesus. The heavenly presence is disturbing to sinful men, but it is a delight to cleansed hearts.

Elisabeth, the mother of John the Baptist, "was filled with the Holy Ghost" (Luke 1:41). Elisabeth heard Mary's greeting and the babe leaped in her womb for joy (v. 44)—John was filled with the Holy Spirit while yet unborn (Luke 1:15). God's presence brings the twin spirits of conviction and celebration, "joy unspeakable and full of glory." The Spirit-filled believer is joyfully attracted to the presence of Christ, while soiled souls are repelled.

The angelic messenger appeared to Mary and told her

she would be the mother of the Messiah. "And Mary said, My soul doth magnify the Lord. And my spirit hath rejoiced in God my Saviour" (Luke 1:46-47). Her soul exalted in the Lord, and her spirit rejoiced. So it is that the pure in heart rejoice at all heavenly contact.

Heartfelt joy is evidence of being under the control of the Holy Spirit. Rejoicing in prayer should be as natural as rejoicing with your most intimate friends. There is a certain release and inner freedom that the rejoicing saint experiences.

"Jesus rejoiced in spirit." In those special times when you are overwhelmed by the goodness of God, follow Jesus' example: give yourself to thanksgiving and praise. As believers we have every reason to rejoice, for we have been drawn "nigh by the blood of Jesus." Because of Calvary we are always within speaking distance of our Lord.

Divine Commission

Jesus received great joy when the humble disciples returned from their appointed journey. Jesus' rejoicing led to thanksgiving for the outworking of the divine plan. Genuine joy comes from being rightly related to the Lord; the accomplishment of His will causes the inner man to rejoice.

Nehemiah tells us, "the joy of the Lord is your strength" (Nehemiah 8:10). Joy is the divine enablement for suffering, service, and serious problems. Certainly Christ rejoiced in God and in the disciples' service. He also rejoiced at the prospect of completing the work of redemption. "Who for the joy that was set before Him endured the cross, despising the shame, and is set down at the right hand of the throne of God" (Hebrews 12:2). Contemplating the ultimate result of a cleansed people and resurrection life for Himself and others, Christ was able to endure the horrors of the Cross. Thus it was joy that gave Christ strength to complete His Father's will.

Divine Perspective

Joy comes when we remember the ultimate intention of God in this universe. The ultimate intention of God is to raise an army of blood-bought believers who through overcoming are made fit to rule and reign with Him in the ages to come. Immediate concerns, circumstances, and conflicts can rob us of joy unless we learn to see life from God's perspective. Behind the scenes, God has a plan to make us like Christ. And believing this causes us to maintain our joy. "Though now ye see him not, yet believing, ye rejoice with joy unspeakable and full of glory" (1 Peter 1:8). We cannot rejoice because all things are good. We rejoice because God is good and will work even the bad things for a constructive purpose if we trust Him.

The Bible puts tremendous emphasis on rejoicing. Someone counted over 550 references to joy and rejoicing in Scripture. Jesus told us, "Ask, and ye shall receive, that your joy may be full" (John 16:24). Obviously God's people need to be "anointed with the oil of gladness."

Rejoicing is not an emotion first; it is a choice. Here is a good way to pray early in the day: "This is the day which the Lord hath made; (I) will rejoice and be glad in it" (Psalm 118:24). This is a great way to get our hearts and minds in tune with God. "I choose to rejoice. I choose to give thanks." Then, as we continue thanking the Lord for specific things, our spirits begin to rejoice. The inner peace and joy will carry us through the day in royal fashion. There will be struggles and times of trial. But the Christian life was never meant to be a continuous pain. Jesus came that we might have abundant life! Rejoicing is to be our way of life.

Chapter 6
RETREAT

And straightway he constrained his disciples to get into the
ship, and to go to the other side before unto Bethsaida, while
he sent away the people. And when he had sent them away,
he departed into a mountain to pray.
—Mark 6:45-46

The multitudes were seeking Jesus. His popularity was
growing. People poured out from the cities to see and hear
Him. As Jesus viewed the vast crowd, His heart was moved
with compassion. They were like sheep without a shepherd.
He taught them many things.

The day was nearly spent. Considering the late hour
and the remote location, the disciples suggested the throngs
be released to go into neighboring villages to buy food.
But Jesus had a different plan. With only five loaves and

two fishes in hand, Jesus commanded the people to sit in groups. A notable miracle then took place—five thousand men were fed. After everyone was satisfied, twelve baskets of bread and fish remained and were taken up.

Jesus then put the disciples on a boat headed for Bethsaida and dismissed the crowds. "And when he had sent them away, he departed into a mountain to pray" (Mark 6:46). This is only one of many times Christ spent praying on a mountainside. The mountains seemed to hold a special attraction for Jesus. After a harried day of activity and involvement with people, the tranquility of the mountain setting allured Him to prayer. Those prayer retreats were normal procedure with Jesus. Earlier in this chapter He had led the disciples to a quiet place to rest after they had returned from a tour of ministry.

Times spent alone with God are not a luxury; they are a necessity if one is to maintain spiritual sanity. After creating the universe in six days, God rested on the seventh. The Old Testament Law required a keeping of the Sabbath, a day when no work was to be done. It was a day for physical rest and spiritual refreshment.

Somehow the idea has come down that busyness is

equivalent to godliness. A great number of people work like mad fifty weeks out of the year so they can take a vacation and relax! Certainly nothing is wrong with vacations. But how much better it would be if we would learn, as Vance Havner suggested, to take "inside vacations" along the way. If we are to stay spiritually sensitive, these inner retreats are mandatory.

A certain missionary employed a group of Africans to help transport his belongings to a distant location. The first day he rushed them on relentlessly because he was already late. The end of the day came, and they all rested their loads on the ground and went to sleep. The next day the missionary came early and directed the Africans to load up so they could get started. They sat silently—nobody moved. The missionary reinforced his command through an interpreter, but the Africans just sat there. In frustration he asked the interpreter why no one was responding. The interpreter answered, "They are waiting for their souls to catch up with their bodies!"

While the Bible emphasizes diligence, it also clearly emphasizes the need to maintain a peaceful inner life. The clearest example is Jesus Himself. He kept a rigorous schedule most of the time, but He always retreated to the place of prayer. If Christ needed quiet retreats alone with God, how much more do we? Rather than getting lost in a flurry of endless activity, we must "allow our souls to catch up with our bodies." We must resolve to break away from our busy schedules to pray.

Jesus left the mountain and walked on the sea, much to the amazement of the troubled disciples who toiled with the oars to steady the ship. Having walked with God on the mountain, Jesus had no problem walking on the stormy sea. He boarded the ship and comforted His disciples. As they arrived at their destination, people again recognized Jesus and began coming to Him for healing. Jesus' retreat to the mountain enabled Him to carry on a ministry of miracles.

Chapter 7
SPECIFICS

Satan hath desired to have you, that he may sift you as
wheat: But I have prayed for thee, that thy faith fail not.
—Luke 22:31-32

Jesus anticipates Peter's need as Satan would soon
launch an all-out attack. The illustration of sifting wheat,
with the violent movement of the sieve and the breaking
up of the wheat, pictures well the violent trial that would
come upon Peter and the disciples once Christ was arrested
and separated from them. Jesus foresees this and responds
by praying specifically for Peter. His prayer is precise, the
object definite. Our Lord requests that an overcoming faith
be given to Peter—faith that would ultimately triumph in
the face of Satan's onslaught. Peter's later denial of Jesus

showed how badly he needed this prayer. Satan entered into Judas and tried to overthrow Peter's faith. But Christ's intercession for Peter got him through this tumultuous trial.

Dull Praying

How different is this specific type of prayer from the many general prayers offered today. Some prayers are so vague that we could never know if they were answered. Take this one for example: "Lord, be with so-and-so." What does this prayer really mean? The Bible tells us that God is omnipresent—everywhere. How foolish to ask God to be somewhere when He is already there! We would do better to ask the Lord to meet a specific need such as, "Lord, may Your Holy Spirit comfort so-and-so during this difficult time." Or "Lord, please protect so-and-so from satanic attack today."

Some churches solicit "unspoken requests" during prayer time. Those who have these particular petitions desire prayer but do not want to share the details publicly. Perhaps there are times when this is appropriate, but generally speaking, if the matter is worth praying for, it should be shared so intelligent prayer can be made. How can we pray for a specific need when we have no idea what the subject is? This type of praying is totally foreign to the Bible. When Paul mentioned prayer in his letters, he was thanking or asking God for definite things.

A certain group of teenagers were surveyed concerning prayer. One of the questions was, "Why don't you spend more time in prayer?" The most common response was that they found prayer "boring." Can you imagine communication with the Creator to be boring? Where do teenagers get such thoughts about prayer? Once you attend several typical prayer meetings where "pray for Aunt Susie's toe" and the "unspoken requests" occupy the majority of the time, you no longer wonder why many think prayer is boring. These meetings are intensely boring! The supernatural work of God is rarely evident in such gatherings. Generally the same requests are made and they are seldom followed by an observable proof of answered prayer.

Once we are saved, we acquire a whole new vocabulary. Seemingly, one of the most popular prayer terms we pick up is "bless" or "blessing." "Please bless my family, and Lord, bless our church . . . We pray Your blessings on Bill . . .". "Bless" is a biblical word, found more frequently in the Old Testament than in the New Testament. The basic idea behind the word is the "bestowal of good." The New Testament reference to "the blessing of bread" is equivalent to giving thanks. What do we really mean when we ask for God's blessing?

How often do we hear prayers made in the plural that should be coming from the individual? "Lord, You know we really need revival." Or sometimes you hear, "Forgive us all our sins." "We" praying is usually our way of preaching to others rather than really talking to God. This type of praying is often little more than a subtle platform for rebuke and for airing our opinions on a given subject. Rather than confronting people face to face, it is easier to communicate our grievances to these people under the guise of prayerful concern.

There are times when "we" praying is valid. But by and large we need to move to the singular, or "I" praying. Very few of us are in any shape to confess someone else's sins, or to tell the Lord what "we all" need. Most need to learn to talk to God on a one-to-one basis. Deal thoroughly with your own needs first. Confess your own sins first. Ask God to search your own heart first. Then as you move on to intercession, be as precise as possible in your petitions for others.

Definite Praying

Jesus said He had prayed for Peter. He prayed for Peter by name and was very pointed in the request: "that thy faith fail not" (Luke 22:32). His prayer for strengthened faith carried Peter through the dark valley of denial. The prayer of Jesus was answered, and Peter became a pillar in the early church.

We need to "doctrine up" our prayer life. Scripture gives clear-cut guidelines on Christian living. These references will aid us in being more direct in prayer. God's Word and the inner promptings of God's Spirit convey God's will in a given situation, enabling us to pray confidently and intelligently.

What definite requests do you have? As you discern the mind of the Lord, take advantage of the Saviour's invitation to "ask, and ye shall receive, that your joy may be full" (John 16:24).

Chapter 8
HONESTY

Father, if thou be willing, remove this cup from me.
—Luke 22:42

The human part of Jesus was shrinking back from Calvary. As He gasped out this prayer, the "cup" of sin seemed unbearable. Jesus knew what lay ahead. It was for this purpose that He had come to earth. Nevertheless, Jesus expressed His heartfelt feelings to God: "If thou be willing . . ." Fortunately for us, Jesus demonstrates down-to-earth, honest, transparent prayer.

Nothing will quench the Holy Spirit like dishonesty with God. Jesus was not afraid to tell the Father His deepest feelings. Nor do we need to be standoffish with God. We need to learn to be honest with Him.

In being honest before God, we must do something Jesus never had to do: confess our sins. Ever since Adam hid from God among the trees of the garden, sinful man has had the built-in tendency to hide from God. We are afraid of revealing our true selves to God. Why? Because deep down we feel God will be disappointed if we tell Him what we have done. Of course, God already knows what we have done. But pride holds man back from admitting his sins. We are more adept at gathering fig leaves than at telling the truth.

Dishonest Praying

We implement all kinds of escape tactics before we learn to own up to our sin. Quite popular today are wholesale confessions like "Lord, forgive me of all my sins." The wholesale approach is like putting all our sins in a bushel basket. The whole transaction takes only about three seconds. Blanket coverage may be available from insurance companies, but blanket confessions achieve absolutely nothing with God. Sins are committed one at a time, and that is the way they must be confessed—one at a time. Specific transgressions require specific admissions.

A second popular approach is the "help me" syndrome.

"Lord, help me to be a better Christian." "Lord, help me not to be impatient." "Lord, help me not to worry." Rather than telling the truth to God and repenting of the last time, we seek His assistance to do better the next time! But God is not interested in being our assistant! He is not interested in being our associate. When Jesus comes into a life, He does not come to help out—He comes to take over! The proper prayer is not "Lord, help me" but "Lord, have me. I have nothing to offer You but failure, but here I am. Have me." It is a humbling thing to acknowledge our failures, but God gives grace to the humble. Our greatest need is to be under the control of the Holy Spirit; He cannot fill our hearts until all sin has been cleansed.

Rededication

Another popular tactic in avoiding honesty is resolving or rededicating. The story is told of a man who overslept and was late for work. When he finally woke up, he realized he was the only one left in the house. He rushed into the bathroom and grabbed a quick shower and shave. He quickly dressed, ran downstairs, and slammed the door.

When he returned that afternoon, he received quite a shock. The whole house was soaked! He had left the water running in the bathroom all day long with the drain plugged. Not bothering to touch the sink, he immediately grabbed a mop and began mopping up the excess water.

Soon his wife and kids came home. His wife stepped onto the soggy living room carpet, dropped two bags of groceries on the floor, and commented, "There's water everywhere!" The husband responded, "That's a good observation. Now grab a mop and start mopping!" They mopped and mopped, but to no avail. Soon the man realized drastic action must be taken if the matter was to be resolved.

He went throughout the neighborhood recruiting all his neighbors for a "bring your own mop party." Soon the house was teeming with eager moppers, but still they couldn't clean up all the water.

Being the good Christian that he was, this man rushed down to the local Christian bookstore and inquired about a book that might help him. The store manager recommended a latest bestseller, *Three Easy Steps to Becoming a Better Mopper*. Quickly the man memorized the three easy steps and enthusiastically related them to the moppers. "Step one: Get a firm grasp on the mop. Step two: Take big, wide strokes. Step three: Work hard, and work fast." They all worked hard and fast, but they could not get all the water up. The three easy steps had failed. More than ever he knew drastic measures had to be taken.

Next he hopped a plane and was gone a whole week to a "Mop Conference." These conferences specialize in techniques on better mopping. Star moppers motivate participants to be the best moppers in their towns. In one of these sessions this man made a decision and resolved to go home and get that water up. However, the emotional rush subsided quickly, and the water was still there.

In sheer desperation he searched the Yellow Pages and invited a professional mop team into his home. The mop team suggested methods and lectured the family on ways to get the water up. As before, this episode failed.

Finally, little Johnny approached his father. "Dad," he said, "I am not trying to tell you what to do, but if you want to get the water up, why don't you go upstairs and turn the faucet off?"

Now that may be a ridiculous story. Yet that is how many of us live as Christians. Rededicating is like mopping up water: It deals with the symptom, not the source. If we want to experience victory in our lives, we must go beyond the fruit all the way to the root. Only severe honesty will admit the faucet is dripping in the bathroom. Though it may be painful, we must be willing to tell God the whole truth. Promises and attempts to do better fail to deal with wrongs already committed.

Peter promised Jesus he would never deny Him. Yet before the cock crowed three times, Peter had cursed and denied Jesus. Peter did not realize his own condition. He did not know how weak he really was. It is useless to make promises we cannot keep.

Years ago our little boy was continually biting his baby brother. At first, I made him apologize and promise not to bite his brother again. But after only a short time he clamped down on his brother again! I finally saw how useless it was to ask my son to make promises he could not keep. When my child does wrong, I don't want promises, I simply want him to say he is sorry. Rededication is an attempt to improve one's self. We need to be dedicated. But if we slip and go back on our dedication, we don't need to rededicate—we need to repent! Repentance involves a thorough confession and a change of our mind and actions. Much of the "rededication" that takes place is only a substitute for genuine repentance.

Honest Praying

God will never let you down, but He will never let you off without telling the truth. God knows the truth about us already. He knew we were going to be the kind of people we are. He anticipated the thoughts we would have and the sins we would commit. Nothing we have to tell Him is going to shock Him; Jesus took the shock of our sins on Calvary.

Honesty is a key ingredient in a meaningful prayer life. Do you tell God exactly how you feel? When you feel apathetic, cold, or unconcerned, you can tell God. If you are not getting anything from your quiet time, stop reading and talk to God. Tell Him you are having a hard time concentrating. The Bible says we can have boldness to approach His throne to find help in time of need. God sent an angel to strengthen Jesus as He agonized in the garden. Likewise, your honesty will release God to minister to your needs.

"Now the Lord is that Spirit: and where the Spirit of the Lord is, there is liberty. But we all with open face beholding as in a glass the glory of the Lord, are changed into the same image from glory to glory, even as by the Spirit of the Lord" (2 Corinthians 3:17-18).

An "open face" is an unveiled face. "If I regard iniquity in my heart, the Lord will not hear me" (Psalm 66:18). In order to be on speaking terms with God, we must be thorough in the area of honest confession. The word "confess" simply means to admit, to agree with, or to say the same thing. "If we confess (or say the same thing God says about) our sins, he is faithful and just to forgive us our sins" (1 John 1:9). Sin blocks our spiritual gaze from seeing God. Honest confession removes the veil so we can contact God.

Rinker says, "Prayer is dialogue between two people who love each other." Meaningful conversation must be gut-level communication. If we are to grow into an intimate relationship with God, we must learn to be honest with God just as Christ our Lord was.

Chapter 9
SOLITUDE

And it came to pass, as he was alone praying,
his disciples were with him.
—Luke 9:18

Read this verse again carefully. Did you catch the apparent contradiction? How could Jesus be alone if the disciples were with Him? Of course, no contradictions exist in Scripture, only misunderstandings about the real meaning.

Jesus was there. The disciples were there. The disciples knew Jesus was there. But Jesus was lost in communion, caught up in unshakable concentration. His preoccupation with the Father overshadowed all else. The disciples were with Jesus, but He was alone with God.

Simplicity

I recall a certain prayer session where the room was packed with believers. In the midst of praying, a certain man cried out, "Lord, I am willing to do anything in order to get right with you, even if I have to go to jail!" That man was alone praying. In true prayer, our awareness of God exceeds our awareness of men. But how often are prayers formed for the ears of men rather than for the heart of God?

Have you been in a prayer meeting, awaiting your turn to pray? As you wait, you contemplate how to begin your prayer. Do you try to think of a remote Scripture text, a catchy combination of words, or a good sentence to begin your prayer so you can impress your listening friends? Whenever this occurs, know for sure you are not "alone praying." For when you really pray, your focus is toward God, not people.

We have all had the experience of being surrounded by people—yet feeling very much alone. We can be in a large crowd and not be in company. When we are praying, whether with a single person or a whole group, we should talk to the Lord as if He were the only one listening. Group prayer should be an extension of private prayer.

Note the simple innocence of a new convert praying, "Lord, this is Bill. You know my heart is cold, and I really didn't feel like attending church today . . ." Isn't it refreshing to hear a young believer talk to God before he has learned all the Christian lingo? How much better to join with a prayer offered with child-like honesty than to repeat the status quo Sunday morning prayer, "Lord, bless the gift and the giver, those that have and those that don't. Save the lost, and heal the sick. In Jesus' name. Amen."

Obviously this sort of prayer is useless. The sick are not all healed, and the lost are not all saved. Not only is it useless, it is harmful. It mesmerizes the congregation, for the prayer is more a demonstration of ritual than of revelation or of relationship to a Holy God. Jesus warned against repeating the same phrases until they lose all meaning. What would be left if all the clichés and catchwords were removed from our prayers? Better to take ten minutes to pray three words with meaning than to rush mindlessly into God's presence babbling a host of empty words.

On several occasions the Bible records Jesus praying in solitary places (Matthew 14:23; Mark 1:35; Luke

5:16; 6:12). These were times of undisturbed, unbroken fellowship. At times He was physically alone, and other times He withdrew for prayer spiritually and mentally amidst the disciples. Whether alone in a crowd or alone Himself, our Lord spent time in the secret presence of God.

Spirituality

Prayer is the acid test of a man's spirituality. Talent, education, and persuasiveness may produce great human results, but only through prayer will we see God's results! Most of our trouble can be traced to poverty in our prayer life.

Some complain that we are out of touch with our generation. The real problem is that we are out of touch with God! In the four Gospels we find repeated and continual references to our Lord's practice of prayer. But in contrast, we must realize that the average minister spends less than five minutes a day in private prayer!

Our society discourages the nourishment of the inner life. Heavy demands are placed on our time by jobs, family responsibilities, and church activities. But our number one priority must be quality time alone with God. Somehow we must distinguish the nonessentials and put first things first. The average church today places more emphasis on softball and aerobics than on prayer! Neglect of the internal relationship with God affects all areas of both the Christian's personal life and the corporate life of the church.

If church members awoke out of their spiritual slumber and took prayer seriously, vitality and renewal would break forth just as it did in the book of Acts.

Today's ministerial student is well equipped with theology, psychology, and sociology. But a good deal of this knowledge could pass for "worldly wisdom." His great lack is experiential knowledge of God. Perhaps this partially accounts for the tremendous instability in our pulpits. Nervous breakdowns and moral failure are now commonplace in the church. Maybe the landslide would subside if congregations and ministers alike agreed that God's messengers were to give themselves "continually to prayer, and to the ministry of the word" (Acts 6:4).

The man who is too busy for prayer is a "practical atheist." If he is too busy for prayer, he is too busy for God. His doctrinal statement may be in order, but his priorities are not. The practice of meditative, contemplative prayer is absolutely essential to maintain spiritual and moral sanity. To be cold in prayer is to be cold in heart. Insensitivity and spiritual dullness are unavoidable apart from time alone with God.

Chapter 10
ALTERATION

And as he prayed, the fashion of his countenance was altered,
and his raiment was white and glistering.
—Luke 9:29

A pastor friend told me he had been praying for revival in his congregation. He shared how he had invested large amounts of time in serious prayer for his church family. After several months of diligent prayer he commented, "God has not yet done anything for my people; but, my, how God has worked me over since I really started praying!"

This brother had discovered a great secret: Prayer is not primarily our way of getting God to change things; prayer is God's way of changing us. The change wrought by prayer is often not seen first in the person for whom prayer is made, but it occurs in the person praying. Someone has said, "There is no place as transforming as the place of prayer."

Our text says that as Jesus was praying His appearance was altered, and His clothes began shining brightly. Here we see the Son of God transfigured. It is significant that this transformation occurred "as He prayed" (v. 29). Now, if Jesus Christ had a "face lift," perhaps we also stand in need of one ourselves! I am not speaking of cosmetic surgery or of a fake plastic smile, but of a renewing work in our hearts that shows on our faces. (If you question the need for this type of change, sit in the choir of the average church next Sunday morning and behold the faces of the congregation or just look at the choir.)

Peter, James, and John were asleep on the mountain at the moment of the Transfiguration. But when they awoke, "they saw his glory" (Luke 9:32). Later, Peter wrote concerning Jesus' transformation: "We . . . were eyewitness of his majesty" (2 Peter 1:16). John's account stated, "We beheld his glory, the glory as of the only begotten of the Father" (John 1:14). No man has ever seen the glorified Christ and remained the same.

"For God, who commanded the light to shine out of darkness, hath shined in our hearts, to give the light of the knowledge of the glory of God in the face of Jesus Christ" (2 Corinthians 4:6).

Paul spoke from experience as he wrote, "Though our outward man perish, yet the inward man is renewed day by day" (2 Corinthians 4:16). The believer needs daily renewal. He needs not only to "have devotions;" he needs to meet God daily on a spiritual level. As he brings his gaze to focus on God, his soul is nourished and refreshed.

Believers often attempt to persuade God to change family members, associates, or circumstances. If the Lord is not changing those for whom we pray, perhaps He wants to change us first. Let God search your motives.

Why do you want God to change your friends or loved ones? Is it so things will go easier for you? Allow God to search your attitudes. Are you responding properly toward those for whom you pray? Do you love them with the love of Christ?

The Lord seldom changes circumstances until circumstances change our character. Recall the time when Paul and Silas were beaten and thrown in jail. Do you remember their response to this mistreatment? They prayed and sang praises at midnight. Evidently, it was as they were praying in those adverse conditions that God sent an earthquake and loosed their bonds! We can learn invaluable lessons from abrasive circumstances and relationships, namely this: God is out to change us, and He will, as we cooperate with Him in the place of prayer.

Prayer brings change primarily in the disposition and perspective. The praying saint is "changed into the same image from glory to glory, even as by the Spirit of the Lord" (2 Corinthians 3:18). As we pray, the Lord transforms our thinking processes to be like His. True prayer replaces false thoughts with right ones. True prayer releases us from the pressures and burdens of life. "Casting all your care upon him; for he careth for you" (1 Peter 5:7). Honest prayer clears the air so the glory of God can be seen. Prayer purifies the heart, frees the mind, and revives the spirit. Prayer brings new perspective.

"Be careful for nothing; but in every thing by prayer and supplication with thanksgiving let your requests be made known unto God. And the peace of God, which passeth all understanding, shall keep your hearts and minds through

Christ Jesus. Finally, brethren, whatsoever things are true . . . honest . . . just . . . pure . . . lovely . . . of good report; if there be any virtue, and if there be any praise, think on these things" (Philippians 4:6-8).

By prayer God enables us to view life from His perspective. Praise replaces griping. Faith displaces doubt. Thanksgiving abounds where once we murmured. With the soul at rest in God through continual prayer, a thorough alteration takes place.

This is not a one-time experience that sets you up for the rest of your life. It is a gradual and progressive alteration. The more clearly one beholds Him, the more deeply he is changed. Thus, we are transfigured into His likeness "from glory to glory." So much emphasis has been placed on the crisis act of believing the finished work of Christ that many have either neglected or misunderstood the continuous work of the Spirit.

Quality time with God in prayer affects moral change. The person praying may not discern the change, but his family members will. The worshipping saint is growing spiritually, and those who know him best are aware of his progress. An increased understanding and knowledge of

God will necessitate change in the life. The alteration of the inner life results in a corresponding change in behavior.

As we see Him and hear Him, we are changed. Prayer and careful study of the Word are the means to hearing His voice and establishing a proper perspective. A change in life then gives an outward expression to internalized truth. "There is no place as transforming as the place of prayer."

Chapter 11
INSTRUCTION

And it came to pass, that, as he was praying in a certain place, when he ceased, one of his disciples said unto him, Lord, teach us to pray...And he said unto them, When ye pray, say, Our Father.
—Luke 11:1-2a

The disciples had observed the Master praying on many occasions. Now they were ready to take the step from being spectators to participating. No longer were they content to watch; they were now ready to be taught how to pray.

Teachableness is one of the greatest traits an individual can possess. Desire and willingness are the basic components of a teachable spirit, and these are the bedrock of all progress and growth in all realms of life. A person must be willing to admit his illness and also have a desire to get well before he will seek out a physician. The student willingly acknowledges that he does not know enough and desires to learn more before he submits to the educational process. Someone said that "marriages were made in heaven, but unfortunately we have to live them out on earth!" If marriages "on earth" are to be pleasurable, they too must be based on willingness and desire.

What is true in medicine, education, and marriage is also true in spiritual growth. We must be willing to acknowledge our need and possess a corresponding desire to get to know God better.

Because of their willingness and desire to grow spiritually, the disciples asked, "Lord, teach us to pray." They did not ask to be taught about prayer; they wanted to know how to pray. They wanted to get involved with God on an intimate, personal basis, not merely an intellectual one.

The disciples were willing for Christ to teach them to pray His way. Are you willing to be taught to pray Jesus' way? You must be willing and desirous to enter Christ's school of prayer. Why not bow your head right now and give God permission to tear down any false notions you have and construct a new attitude in your heart about prayer?

Petition

Jesus' instructional prayer in Matthew 6 begins, "After this manner therefore pray" (v. 9). Since preceding verses warn of using vain repetitions, Jesus obviously did not intend for this prayer to be repeated as some divine formula; it is instead a fashion of prayer to be followed. This model prayer of petition, or asking, is divided into segments of three requests for God's glory followed by four requests for man's need. This order must be more than coincidence; God's concerns rightly come first, and then man's.

The first three phrases recognize God's greatness and authority:

"Hallowed (honored) be Thy name"

"Thy kingdom come"

"Thy will be done"

The remaining requests deal with our total dependency:

"Give us this day our daily bread"

"Forgive us our debts"

"Lead us not into temptation"

"Deliver us from evil"

The first three requests set the tone for the other requests. All true prayers of petition will accomplish these primary objectives: (1) they will honor God; (2) they will seek to advance His kingdom; (3) they will be submissive to His will. The human aspect will always fall in line if these three criteria are met.

The "Unknown Christian" said, "Prayer is not man's way of getting his will done in heaven. Prayer is God's way of getting His will done on earth." We do not order God to do our will in our prayers; rather, through prayer, we are enabled to do His will. We do not pray in order to persuade God to take our viewpoint; prayer changes our disposition to see God's vantage point.

The spirit in which Jesus taught us to pray is significant:

"Our Father"—a family spirit

"Hallowed be Thy name" —a reverential spirit

"Thy kingdom come"—a loyal spirit

"Thy will be done"—a submissive spirit

"Give us . . . our daily bread"—a dependent spirit

"Forgive us our debts as we forgive our debtors"—a

confessing and forgiving spirit

"Deliver us from evil"—a humble spirit

"Thine is the kingdom"—an adoring spirit

Jesus' sample prayer encompasses all of life. Its wording embraces God, others, and ourselves in relation to them. "Our Father" is a child addressing his divine Parent. "Hallowed be Thy name" is a worshipper exalting his God. "Thy kingdom come" is a subject appealing to his King. "Thy will be done" is a servant praying to his Master. "Give us this day our daily bread" is a dependent soliciting his Provider. "Forgive us our debts" is a sinner pleading mercy from his Saviour. "And lead us not into temptation, but deliver us from evil" is a pilgrim talking to his Guide. We should pray a prayer of this type slowly, pausing at every thought, until we grasp its true meaning.

An evangelist was holding services in a certain town. Not much was happening, very few were being saved. The evangelist heard that Praying Hyde was visiting town, so he made an appointment to pray with Mr. Hyde. The evangelist prayed fervently for about five minutes, pouring out his heart to God. Upon finishing, he waited for Praying Hyde to pray. Nothing but silence followed as they waited on their faces before God. After what seemed to be a long period of time, Mr. Hyde managed to utter in a strained manner the words, "Oh, God." The meaning began to sink deep into the heart of the evangelist as he waited for another extended period of time in which Hyde did not say another word. At length, Praying Hyde gasped out again, "Oh, God." At that very instant the evangelist knew God was in their midst, and the desired breakthrough in the meetings had come. How important it is to pray so that every word has meaning, rather than rehearsing a barrage of rapid-fire words that are barely understood before they are uttered!

Practical

God is concerned with the whole of life, and all of life is touched in Jesus' prayer. "Bread" has to do with physical needs. "Forgive us" deals with the mental aspects of guilt and anguish. "Deliver us from evil" addresses spiritual concerns. "Thy will be done" relates to the will, and choices in life.

This instructional prayer is intensely practical. The Lord tells us to "say" or "speak" when we pray. This is not mere meditation. Prayer is to be spoken aloud. Our minds tend to wander when we pray silently. Speaking out loud helps us to concentrate and keep our minds in step with the things our mouths are speaking. Sometimes silent prayer is necessary when we are surrounded by people. But we need times alone with God in which verbal communication is employed.

Another benefit of praying aloud is that we develop a deeper awareness of God's presence. Focusing on God as the One we are addressing helps shut out self-consciousness. The mind and heart center on God's Person. We sense His presence and become aware of His nearness.

We do not need to be quotable or fancy in prayer. Many complain, "I wish I could pray better public prayers." This really misses the whole point. The soul of the matter of prayer is simply verbalizing the intents of one's heart regardless of the language or the flow of words. One should address God with reverence, but one does not have to pray in Old English! "Thee," "Thou," "blessest," etc. are fine, but who uses those words in conversing with the grocer? Speak with the Lord in your everyday language.

Personal

The word "Father" denotes affection, a family term.

Jesus addressed God as "Father." Furthermore, He instructs us to call God "Father" also. Think of it. The Father of Jesus Christ is now our Father as well! Because of Calvary we now have access to God's throne—not as an enemy, or even as a servant, but as His child. A certain minister began his prayer, "My Father." The words so gripped his heart he could not proceed until his soul had absorbed all possible meaning from his salutation, "My Father."

How thankful we ought to be for the teaching our Lord has given us on prayer. He not only tells us what to do; He also shows us how to do it. However, prayer is never purely an academic exercise. True prayer is born of the Holy Spirit. Our great need is to develop sensitivity to the inner promptings of God's Spirit. We need proper understanding of prayer as well as the filling, or control, of the Holy Spirit.

Why not take some time praying as Jesus taught us? Linger at each point, and allow God to saturate your mind with His thoughts. Humble yourself under His mighty hand regularly, and allow the gentle Comforter to teach you to pray just as Christ taught His disciples to pray.

Chapter 12

REFUGE

And in the morning, rising up a great while before day,
he went out, and departed into a solitary place,
and there prayed.
—Mark 1:35

The previous day had been extremely busy for Jesus. In fact, all the city had gathered at the door of the house where He was staying because many had been healed and delivered from evil spirits. But early in the morning, Jesus ventured out to a quiet place for prayer. On many occasions, in the midst of the pressures of public ministry, Jesus sought refuge in the solitary place. Jesus knew little of the need for recreation and relaxation emphasized today. A change of scenery can be beneficial, but Jesus found that altering His spiritual gaze toward the Father was more than adequate. There in the place of quiet refuge, Jesus prayed.

Jesus learned to find real rest in the solitary place. There human faculties find tremendous release. Today Jesus invites us to take refuge in Him: "Come unto me, all ye that labour and are heavy laden, and I will give you rest" (Matthew 11:28). Rest in our souls is attained simply by coming to Jesus and quieting our hearts in His presence. Still, many are not willing to discipline themselves in this manner.

Soon after Jesus departed that morning, Peter and several disciples went out and searched for Jesus. They tracked Him down and came upon Him as He quietly prayed. Peter blurted out, "All men seek for thee" (Mark 1:37). Having witnessed the miracles on the previous day, the multitudes were anxious to see Him again. But the Master decisively responded, "Let us go into the next towns" (v. 38).

The pathway to ministry is made known in prayer. Jesus refused to be distracted from His divine mission. Maintaining communion with His Father was more important than anything else. Though the multitudes were seeking Him, He could not be deterred from carrying out His Father's will. A great lesson can be gleaned here. Obedience ruled the life of Jesus—not pressure from men. Accomplishing God's will was the supreme rule for Christ, even if it disappointed those desiring to see Him. Jesus often departed from the multitudes to commune with His Father.

To spend a whole night or the greater part of the night, hidden away in prayer was Jesus' way of preparing Himself for preaching, performing miracles, and discovering His Father's will in important decisions. Prayer clears the vision, gives mental poise, steadies the nerves, sweetens the spirit, and strengthens the heart. Busy days are times when the morning watch must be carefully guarded.

"And when he had sent the multitudes away, he went up into a mountain apart to pray: and when the evening was come, he was there alone" (Matthew 14:23). Everything has its time—a time for people, a time to be alone, and a time exclusively for prayer. To avoid distraction, Jesus sent the crowds on their way. Many times Christ draws us to Himself. On these occasions we must learn to dismiss the distractions and follow the attraction to the place of prayer.

This may be harder to do than it seems.

I recall a prayer meeting in which several men had gathered to pray. In the midst of prayer the phone rang. No less than three men sprang from their knees to answer the phone. Our impulsive reflexes are in better shape than our inner lives! The average believer is easily distracted from prayer by a phone call, a crying baby, an urgent matter. If the phone rings while we are talking to another human being, at least we have the courtesy to say, "Excuse me." Imagine how God must feel when the slightest distraction grabs our attention without so much as "Pardon me for a moment!"

The tendency in our day is to cater to men instead of communing with God. The mad rush for counseling exposes the fact that advice from men is often more highly esteemed than guidance from God. Without question, many believers need counsel, and Scripture makes clear, "In the multitude of counsellors there is safety" (Proverbs 11:14). But praying people learn to acquire wisdom from God. "If any of you lack wisdom, let him ask of God" (James 1:5). Have you learned the secret of divine guidance? There is no substitute for time alone with God. Paul's Christianity was born in prayer: "Lord, what wilt thou have me to do?" After his conversion, Paul did not immediately confer "with flesh and blood" (Galatians 1:16). He knew the greatest resource—access to God Himself—is available to all who are "in Christ."

These are busy days for most of us, so taking time for prayer must become a settled priority. Nothing is more important in our fast-paced society than finding daily refuge in prayer. We find the secret to fruitful life and ministry in our Lord's habits.

Chapter 13
INTERCESSION

I pray for them.
—John 17:9

The longest recorded prayer of Christ is found in John 17. Matthew Henry said, "This is a prayer after a sermon. When He had spoken from God to them, He turned to speak to God for them." Many of Christ's prayers could be termed intercessory; however, John 17 is the best example of this type of prayer.

To intercede means to "beseech on behalf of another." Therefore, intercessory prayer is fervently petitioning God for someone other than ourselves. Jesus prayed for little children. Mark tells us that "he took them up in his arms, put his hands upon them, and blessed them" (Mark

10:16). Another reference, Matthew 19:13, reads: "Then were there brought unto him little children, that he should put his hands on them, and pray." Jesus also prayed for Peter, because Satan desired to violently "sift" him. Jesus even prayed for those who crucified Him, saying, "Father, forgive them." Christ often prayed for others.

In John 17:1-5, Jesus prays for Himself. Then He prays for His disciples in verses 6-19, and in verses 20-26 He prays for all believers.

Himself

These words spake Jesus, and lifted up his eyes to heaven, and said, Father, the hour is come; glorify thy Son, that thy Son also may glorify thee:

As thou hast given him power over all flesh, that he should give eternal life to as many as thou hast given him.

And this is life eternal, that they might know thee the only true God, and Jesus Christ, whom thou hast sent.

I have glorified thee on the earth: I have finished the work which thou gavest me to do.

And now, O Father, glorify thou me with thine

own self with the glory which I had with thee before the world was (John 17:1-5).

Christ prayed for Himself first. His first petition is that the Father would glorify Him—so He could glorify the Father. We are not wrong to pray for God's blessing when our motivation is pure. The psalmist prayed, "I will run the way of thy commandments, when thou shalt enlarge my heart" (Psalm 119:32). To put it another way, "I will do Your will as You give me the capacity." This is the heart of Jesus' opening request, "Glorify thy Son, that thy Son also may glorify thee."

He talks about His earthly mission in verses 2-4 and reiterates His request in the fifth verse: "Glorify thou me." Then He moves on to intercede for His followers.

The Disciples

I have manifested thy name unto the men which thou gavest me out of the world: thine they were, and thou gavest them me; and they have kept thy word.

Now they have known that all things whatsoever thou hast given me are of thee.

For I have given unto them the words which

thou gavest me; and they have received them, and have known surely that I came out from thee, and they have believed that thou didst send me.

I pray for them: I pray not for the world, but for them which thou hast given me; for they are thine.

And all mine are thine, and thine are mine; and I am glorified in them.

And now I am no more in the world, but these are in the world, and I come to thee. Holy Father, keep through thine own name those whom thou hast given me, that they may be one, as we are.

While I was with them in the world, I kept them in thy name: those that thou gavest me I have kept, and none of them is lost, but the son of perdition; that the scripture might be fulfilled.

And now come I to thee; and these things I speak in the world, that they might have my joy fulfilled in themselves.

I have given them thy word; and the world hath hated them; because they are not of the world, even as I am not of the world.

I pray not that thou shouldest take them out of the world, but that thou shouldest keep them from the evil.

They are not of the world, even as I am not of the world.

Sanctify them through thy truth; thy word is truth.

As thou hast sent me into the world, even so I have also sent them into the world.

And for their sakes I sanctify myself, that they also might be sanctified through the truth (John 17:6-19).

This portion of the prayer is exclusive. The phrase "those thou gavest me" or a similar expression is found twice in verse 6 and once in verses 9, 11, and 12. He viewed the disciples as God's gift to Him.

Jesus did not pray for two things. "I pray not for the world" (v. 9). First, His prayer was not a general request for all humanity; it was specific intercession for His friends. This is not a prayer for world peace or reclamation of the world system. It would take the tragedy of the Cross to redeem this fallen world. Jesus is praying specifically for

His disciples. Jesus also did not ask God to "take them out of the world, but that thou shouldest keep them from the evil" (v. 15). Just as He had been sent into the world, Jesus "sent them into the world" (v. 18). The disciples had a mission, just like Jesus. They were sent to proclaim the good news. This was their date with destiny, and Jesus prays that they may be kept safe on the right path.

Having stated He was not praying for the world or for the removal of the disciples from the world, Jesus requested five things for the disciples. First, He prayed that they might be securely kept: "Keep through thine own name those whom thou has given me" (v. 11). Second, Jesus prayed for them to be unified: "that they may be one, as we are" (v. 11). Next, Jesus prayed "that they might have my joy fulfilled in themselves" (v. 13). Then, He prayed for their deliverance from satanic scheming: "keep them from the evil," or the evil one (v. 15). Finally, He interceded for their sanctification, or that they be made pure and holy: "Sanctify them through thy truth" (v. 17). Christ prayed carefully and thoroughly for His followers. His prayer touched the aspects of continued growth (sanctification), deliverance from Satan, abounding joy, unity, and security.

Future Believers

Neither pray I for these alone, but for them also which shall believe on me through their word;

That they all may be one; as thou, Father, art in me, and I in thee, that they also may be one in us: that the world may believe that thou hast sent me.

And the glory which thou gavest me I have given them; that they may be one, even as we are one:

I in them, and thou in me, that they may be made perfect in one; and that the world may know that thou hast sent me, and hast loved them, as thou hast loved me.

Father, I will that they also, whom thou hast given me, be with me where I am; that they may behold my glory, which thou hast given me: for thou lovedst me before the foundation of the world.

O righteous Father, the world hath not known thee: but I have known thee, and these have known that thou hast sent me. And I have declared unto them thy name, and will declare it: that the love wherewith thou hast loved me may be in them, and

I in them (John 17:20-26).

This part of Jesus' prayer is for those who in the future would become Christians. His first request is for their oneness: "That they all may be one" (v. 21). This phrase appears four times in verses 21-23. How concerned He is for their unity! The unity Christ desired is not enforced by law or mutual enthusiasm. Neither is it a unity which demands compromising the truth. It is a unity which is bound up in Him: "I in them, and thou in me" (v. 23). This oneness is a union of all believers to the Godhead through Christ Himself. The Scripture speaks often of being "in Christ." This oneness of believers both with God and with each other is meant to produce a living witness to the watching world—"that the world may know that thou has sent me" (v. 23). Christians are called upon to demonstrate such unity that a fragmented world will take note and give heed to the reality of Christ's Incarnation as the Son of God.

In verse 23 Jesus asks that "they may be made perfect in one," or perfected in unity. He desires for Christians to grow in grace and knowledge and become stable, mature,

Spirit-led Christians. He intercedes for our completeness—
our growth in Christ.

Jesus mentions our glorification in verses 22 and 24. Jesus
shared His glory with us, and ultimately we will be united
physically with Him to behold His glory! He prayed that we
might be with Him. We are already united spiritually, for
God "hath raised us up together, and made us sit together
in heavenly places in Christ Jesus" (Ephesians 2:6). Our
physical union is guaranteed because Jesus prayed for it and
paid the price to accomplish it!

Our Lord's intercession in this one prayer serves to make
us aware of His present intercessions for us in glory. He is
our Advocate before the Father. He prays with us and for
us. Realizing that Jesus is now praying for us will cause fears
and anxieties to subside. But our Lord's intercessions are a
rebuke as well. His prayers rebuke our chronic prayerlessness
and condemn our self-centered praying. In light of His
intercessions, what enlargement is needed in the breadth and
intensity of our intercessions! We read in Isaiah 59:16 that
the Lord "wondered that there was no intercessor." Do you
not imagine our Lord is even more perplexed at the lack of
heartfelt intercession among the saints in this age of grace?

Cooperating with Jesus

In every sense, Jesus was an intercessor. He stood in the gap and redeemed us to God. He continues to intercede for the saints at the Father's right hand. Herbert Lockyer, in the book *All the Prayers of the Bible*, identifies three essential qualities of a prevailing intercessor.

There are three things an intercessor must remember if his prayers for others are to prevail:

1) He must have a sincere desire for the highest interests of those for whom he prays.

2) He must have the utmost confidence in divine promise and sufficiency to meet the need.

3) He must hold himself in readiness to cooperate in action as an outcome of his intercession.

Christ fulfilled all these requirements and seeks those who will join with Him now in the ministry of intercession. Will you accept His invitation?

While Jesus agonized in the garden, the disciples slept. Jesus returned from praying and said, "Could ye not watch with me for one hour?" Twice more He went off to pray and returned only to find the disciples still sleeping. Upon finding them sleeping the third time He said, "Are you still sleeping and taking your rest?" Could it be that Jesus is asking the same question of us?

The ministry of intercession is sorely needed in these days of casual Christianity. "Are you still sleeping and taking your rest?"

Chapter 14
GROANING

When Jesus therefore saw her weeping…
he groaned in the spirit, and was troubled.
—John 11:33

Lazarus was dead. Mary and Martha were grieving over the loss of their brother. Both said the same words to Jesus, "Lord, if thou hadst been here, my brother had not died" (John 11:21,32). They believed Jesus was the Christ and knew He had the power to prevent death. But He had been absent, and Lazarus was dead.

Death is hard. Overwhelming emotions of sorrow and grief are common in its wake. "When Jesus therefore saw her weeping, and the Jews also weeping which came with her, He groaned in the spirit, and was troubled" (v. 33).

The Master inquired as to the location of the grave. Then Jesus wept. The implication is that He wept angrily as He witnessed the awful consequences of sin upon the human race. Death was not part of the original creation. Death and the grief it causes came as a consequence of man's rebellion.

"Jesus therefore again groaning in himself cometh to the grave" (v. 38). Having become a man, our Lord was troubled with the powerful sentiment of human loss. As they moved the stone, "Jesus lifted up his eyes and said, Father, I thank thee that thou hast heard me" (v. 41). The surge of deep sorrow had overflowed into prayer. Often profound sorrow or joy turn us away from prayer; not so with Christ. "And when He thus had spoken, he cried with a loud voice, Lazarus, come forth" (v. 43). And Lazarus obeyed.

At another time in Christ's ministry, a deaf mute was brought to Him. "And looking up to heaven He sighed," or groaned again (Mark 7:34). Perhaps this was a sigh of sympathy for the handicapped man. But Christ had more than human sympathy, when He stood "looking up to heaven." His compassion for the man led to prayer, and the man was completely healed.

Soon after this, the Pharisees came seeking a sign from heaven (a miracle). "And he sighed deeply in his spirit, and saith, Why doth this generation seek after a sign?" (Mark 8:12). The unbelief of these religious leaders caused Him to groan in His spirit. Then He left them and boarded a ship. Though we are not told what happened aboard the ship, perhaps there He prayed for these blind leaders. Suffering humanity and unbelieving hearts caused His anguished soul to send unutterable sighs and prayers to the Father. Likewise, the blowing winds and gusts of emotion that blow upon our spirits should never interrupt our communion with God. Rather they should contribute to our fellowship with Him, being translated into "supplications with strong crying and tears" (Hebrews 5:7).

Knowing that His death was imminent, Jesus exclaimed, "Now is my soul troubled" (John 12:27). Mere positive thinking, as we understand it today, could not relieve Him. Reality was much too harsh to whitewash with a superficial grin. He was about to bear our sins in His own body. The thought brought a crushing blow to His spirit. Again these intense emotions of spiritual conflict caused Him to pray. He cried, "Father, glorify thy name" (v. 28). The goal of all true prayer is to glorify God. Even while passing through the shadow of death, Jesus prayed for God's glory!

Jesus' "groanings" and "sighs" speak louder than words. Life is not a long, continuous smile. In a broken world like ours we have much to weep about. Human loss, calloused hearts, and tragedy cause us to sigh. But like Christ, we must pray and not faint. We are called to rejoice with those who rejoice and to weep with the weeping ones. However, we must never stop at the tears. We must go beyond the emotions and lift our eyes toward heaven, looking to Him Who alone can comfort and give grace to help in time of need. As the Scripture says, "Casting all your care upon him; for he careth for you" (1 Peter 5:7).

"For we have not an high priest which can not be touched with the feeling of our infirmities; but was in all points tempted (tested) like as we are, yet without sin" (Hebrews 4:15).

Not only did He bear your burden, He bore the burden of the entire world. "Surely he hath borne our griefs, and carried our sorrows" (Isaiah 53:4). Call upon Him in your hour of difficulty, and He will deliver you!

Chapter 15

INTENSITY

And being in an agony he prayed more earnestly:
and his sweat was as it were great drops of
blood falling down to the ground.
—Luke 22:44

Praying was no light thing with Christ. The night He was betrayed, Jesus took three disciples with Him to the garden of Gethsemane and told them to pray. He went on a little further, and an awful struggle ensued. He Who knew no sin was about to become sin for us. The terrific strain of His mental agony was too much for His physical frame to bear. His sweat became mingled with blood, as the text reads, "And his sweat was as it were great drops of blood" (Luke 22:44).

Jesus was undergoing tremendous inner turmoil. The

contemplation of "the cup" was overwhelming. He begged God, "If thou be willing, remove this cup from me" (v. 42). The trauma of Calvary caused physical repercussions. Redemption hinged on His next twenty-four hours. So awful was the battle that a heavenly messenger appeared, "strengthening him" (v. 43). Even after this He was stretched out on His face, "praying more earnestly" (v. 44).

Jesus wrestled in prayer. He agonized and labored in prayer, as we read in Hebrews 5:7:

"Who in the days of his flesh, when he had offered up prayers and supplications with strong crying and tears unto him that was able to save him from death."

No doubt this is a direct reference to Gethsemane, but it may also refer to other strivings of spirit. Christ had intense seasons of prayer. His whole being was involved—his mind, will, and emotions.

Even in the midst of unbearable pressure, Christ never rebelled against God's will. When He said, "If thou be willing, remove this cup from me," He qualified that request by saying "nevertheless not my will, but thine, be done" (Luke 22:42). He never once went against the Father, though He did appeal to the Father's affection and power by asking if the Cross was indispensable. In essence He was asking if there was another means of accomplishing the divine plan. For Christ, prayer was not spoken to change God's will; it was His way to discover the exact will of God. It has been said, "Real prayer is absolute self-surrender to and absolute correspondence with, the mind, the will, the character of God."

How often do we let stress and difficulty cause us to worry and faint spiritually. Jesus responded to extreme pressure by praying. If we are not praying during the good times, how can we hope to discern God's will in the hard times? We must live on praying ground all the time so there is never a need to get "caught up" when the difficulties come.

By studying Christ's life, one readily sees that He was earnest in prayer; He was deeply involved in the vital ministry of prayer. But His labor in prayer stands in sharp contrast to His ease in ministry. Apparently, ministering to people did not exhaust Jesus. Whether He was casting out demons or performing miracles like feeding the five thousand, ministering did not seem to put a strain upon Him. In fact, Jesus often sat down and taught the people.

No theatrics. No dramatic presentation. No hopping around in order to keep the attention of the audience. He never sought to entertain by the way He spoke. Jesus spoke as One Who had authority. The people's minds were attentive to His content, not to the way He presented it. After speaking from a sitting position, He was probably not tired, much less exhausted. Jesus appeared to be relaxed in ministry and intense in prayer. We in the twentieth century tend to be the opposite: intense in ministry and relaxed in prayer! Some of us are so busy for Jesus that we have no time with Jesus. Christ labored in prayer and ministered smoothly. Some of us tend to labor in ministry and pray smoothly.

Although every prayer cannot be intense, there must be times of deep, forceful prayer. Our shallow thoughts of God—based on shallow teaching—make us prone to superficiality. But God desires to deal deeply and thoroughly in our hearts. This is the way to keep the fires of spiritual passion burning.

Where are the agonizers today? Where are those who dare stir themselves up to take hold of God? Where are the ones who will enter into fellowship with Jesus in "strong cryings and tears?" A Christian leader was asked the secret of building a church. He responded, "Bent knees, broken hearts, and wet eyes."

God has chosen to coordinate His will on earth through our prayers. This is one reason Scripture calls us "co-laborers" with God. There is a time to pray and a time to act. We are to be in a spirit of prayer at all times, and there must be seasons when we do nothing but pray.

Prayer is a secret ministry. When you begin to pray in earnest, you probably will not make the religious headlines. But you will play a vital part in fulfilling God's plan, for "the effectual fervent prayer of a righteous man availeth much" (James 5:16). God, give us fervency in our praying!

Chapter 16

RECOGNITION

As he sat at meat with them, he took bread, and blessed it…
And their eyes were opened, and they knew him.
—Luke 24:30-31

It was a sad day for the disciples. Their leader, Jesus, had been crucified. Two of them had left Jerusalem for Emmaus. Along the journey they discussed the tragedy of the preceding days. They had hoped Jesus would redeem Israel and set up a political kingdom, but their hopes were crushed when the chief priests delivered Him to death. Confused and discouraged, they tried to reason it out. What went wrong?

"And it came to pass, that, while they communed together and reasoned, Jesus himself drew near, and went with them. But their eyes were holden that they should not know him" (Luke 24:15-16).

How often Jesus draws near in the troublesome times! But the disciples were so preoccupied with their grievous circumstances that they could not see Jesus, though He was right there with them.

Jesus engaged in conversation with them. Beginning with the events of the crucifixion to the empty tomb, the disciples shared their perplexity. The women at the grave had spoken with an angel who said Jesus was alive. Certain disciples went to inspect the tomb. It was empty, "but him they saw not" (Luke 24:24). At this point Jesus rebuked the disciples sharply for their unbelief and expounded the Scriptures concerning Himself. But after all that Bible study, the disciples were still in the dark. Spiritual truth enters through the mind, but it is revealed primarily by the Spirit. Still they did not know Him.

Then, "he took bread, and blessed it . . . And their eyes were opened, and they knew him" (vv. 30-31). Their hearts were stirred by His teaching, but the veil was lifted when He prayed.

Prayer and the vision of God are bound up together.

And as we envision Christ interceding for us, we too are enabled to pray. A.A. Bonar said, "I would never lose sight of any hour of the Lamb in the midst of the throne, and if I have this sight I shall be able to pray." This vision of God makes life a **continuous** prayer.

We have seen how the Lord lived in an atmosphere of prayer. He was thoroughly saturated and absorbed in prayer. Prayer was to Jesus as air is to the lung—His very breath. And fortunately for us, the Lord Jesus is still praying! Calvary did not end His prayers. He rose again, and ascended to heaven where He is seated at the Father's right hand. There He "ever liveth to make intercession" (Hebrews 7:25). Some imagine that Christ occupies Himself by constructing mansions for the saints. He did say, "I go to prepare a place for you" (John 14:2). However, He spoke the universe into existence. And if He spoke creation into being, preparing heaven for us is not a time-consuming task. Intercession is His main occupation in relation to the church. We Christians have every reason to be encouraged by our Lord's continual prayers. He became Incarnate once. He died once. He rose from the dead once. These are all important. But Jesus has invested the last two millenniums praying. Before His Incarnation He prayed; Scripture says the Father, Son, and Holy Spirit had communion. His earthly life was devoted to prayer. And now His ascended life is devoted to prayer as well.

Perhaps no one cares enough to pray for you. That's doubtful, but even if no one else prays for you, Christ is praying for you. And without doubt, His prayers are heard! And Jesus is not the only One praying for believers. "Likewise the Spirit . . . itself maketh intercession for us with groanings which cannot be uttered" (Romans 8:26). Two Persons of the Godhead are praying for us, and the third hears their prayers. If the Lord is for us, who can be against us?

Chapter 17

IMPACT

Lord, teach us to pray.
—Luke 11:1

Jesus' teaching was great! His miracles were fascinating; His wisdom unparalleled; His power was astounding; and His presence was awesome. Without question, the disciples were impressed by every aspect of Jesus' life. But never did they ask, "Lord, teach us to preach," or "teach us to do miracles." But, having heard Jesus pray, they said, "Lord, teach us to pray."

His prayers left them spellbound. They admitted they were ignorant of how to pray. This is the place for all of us to begin, "for we know not what we should pray for as we ought" (Romans 8:26).

One of the best ways to learn is by observation. We have watched Jesus pray in the preceding pages. In every circumstance, whether in joy or sadness, publicly or privately, we have witnessed the Son of Man praying. Hopefully, watching Jesus pray will affect you as it did the disciples. Are you willing to pray, Lord, teach me to pray? This is not a one-time exercise. Rather we must daily spend time alone with God and ask repeatedly to be schooled in the exercise of genuine prayer.

"Men ought always to pray, and not to faint" (Luke 18:1). If you are fainting, you are not praying, If you are praying, you are not fainting. It is impossible to do both simultaneously. Jesus' life provides the example, and His Word gives the command. We learn by watching and doing. Ultimately, we must engage in actual praying if we are to learn to pray. Talk to God in your own words. Open up and be honest with God. Regular Bible study and time spent alone with God gives Jesus the opportunity to teach you. This is the school of prayer. Anyone who desires may enroll.

Christ's abundant prayer life is overwhelming! Don't be discouraged at the low state of your own. The best teacher you could have is living inside you—the Holy Spirit. "When He, the Spirit of truth, is come, He will guide you into all truth" (John 16:13). This indwelling Person is the Spirit of Prayer.

A CONDENSED SUMMARY OF CHRIST'S PRACTICE OF PRAYER

His prayers at the great events of His life:

    (a) His Baptism [Luke 3:21]

    (b) The choice of the Twelve [Luke 6:12]

    (c) The confession of His Messiahship at Caesarea Philippi [Luke 9:18]

    (d) The Transfiguration [Luke 9:29]

    (e) In Gethsemane [Luke 22:39-46]

    (f) On the Cross [Luke 23:46]

His prayers in the course of His ministry:

    (a) Before the great conflict with the ecclesiastical authorities [Luke 5:16]

    (b) Before giving the Lord's Prayer [Luke 11:1]

    (c) When the Greeks came to Him [John 12:27]

    (d) His retiring after feeding the five thousand [Mark 6:46]

His prayers at His miracles:

    (a) Healing the multitudes [Mark 1:35]

    (b) Feeding the five thousand [Mark 6:41]

(c) Healing a deaf mute [Mark 7:34]

(d) Raising Lazarus [John 11:41]

His prayers for others:

(a) For the Eleven [John 17:6-19]

(b) For the whole Church [John 17:20-26]

(c) For those who nailed Him to the Cross
[Luke 23:34]

(d) For Peter [Luke 22:32]

ABOUT THE AUTHOR

Harold Vaughan is involved in a full-time revival ministry across America, having already ministered in forty-seven states as well as in foreign countries.

Revival in individual lives and the corporate life of the church is the dominant burden of his heart. His ministry is characterized by an emphasis on the abundant life for the believer. He believes that the abundant life is obtained through an exchanged life "Christ's life for your life"— thereby initiating revival among God's people.

Check Out These Other **Helpful Resources**

OUR FAMILY TIME WITH GOD
Compiled by
Harold Vaughan

Written with today's Christian family in mind, the devotional features 365 readings on a variety of topics, including prayer, holiness, God's Word, biblical friendship, God's will, separation, witnessing, trials, worship, joy, biblical authorities, time management, a clear conscience, and the Ten Commandments. Authors representing a variety of ministries from across the country include Harold Vaughan, Tom Palmer, Jack Palmer, Tom Farrell, and others.

Whether gathered around the supper table or in the living room before bedtime, families will enjoy learning biblical truths in an enjoyable, easy-to-read format. *Our Family Time with God* is the ideal resource for parents who want to build a God-centered home.

FORGIVENESS: How to Get Along With Everybody All the Time!
by Harold Vaughan and T.P. Johnston

"In a world filled with so much hatred and misunderstanding, few subjects are as timely as forgiveness. And yet, few works of biblical accuracy have been written on this important subject. Vaughan and Johnston's book is the best, purest and most practical treatment of the subject I know. Everyone who has been forgiven should read this book to know how and why to forgive."
—Woodrow Kroll, *Back to the Bible*

WHAT IT MEANS TO BE CRUCIFIED WITH CHRIST
by Harold Vaughan

What did Paul mean in Galatians 2:20: "I am crucified with Christ"? Here are twelve brief and readable chapters on the "exchanged life" along with many helpful charts and study guides.

THE NATURE OF A GOD-SENT REVIVAL
by Duncan Campbell

Will it be business as usual or the usual business of revival? This powerful booklet is packed with power from a man who saw spiritual awakening in his ministry. Thousands were converted when God stepped down from heaven in the Hebrides.

TIME WITH GOD
by Harold Vaughan

Would you like to read through the entire Bible in just one year? Are you interested in a tool that will assist you in organizing your Bible study? Do you desire to help your family develop the daily discipline of studying God's Word? If you answered "Yes" to any of the above questions, then *Time with God* is the answer. *Time with God* provides you with a reasonable reading schedule that will get you through the Scriptures in a single year. It also will assist you in contemplating the Word by furnishing space to record your thoughts each day. Accountability is another great benefit when the entire family is working through the *Time with God* diary. Whatever your age, you can begin studying to show yourself approved TODAY!

✝Christ Life
PUBLICATIONS

Christ Life Ministries is committed to providing messages, materials, and ministries that will further revival, both personally and corporately, in the local church.

- Spiritual Life Crusades
- Prayer Advances
- Christ Life Publications

Visit our website
www.christlifemin.org

- Read thought-provoking articles.

- Learn about the Prayer Advances for men, ladies, students, and couples.

- Sign up for our online newsletter.

- Listen to audio sermons.

- Review publications and resources that will help you and your family.

- Learn more about Christ Life Ministries.

Quantity Discounts!

Christ Life Publications offers special discounts to persons, churches, and distributors who buy *"The Prayer Life of Jesus"* in bulk quantities. See Order Form on the reverse of this page.

O R D E R   F O R M

Quantity Prices for "The Prayer Life of Jesus"

1-5 Copies $6.99 each
6-10 Copies $5.99 each

11-49 Copies $4.99 each
50 or More Copies $4.00 each
(prices are subject to change.)

QTY _____ "The Prayer Life of Jesus" $ _____
Shipping & Handling $ _____
VA residents add 5% sales tax $ _____
Total $ _____

Shipping & Handling (Continental USA only & subject to change)

Under $25.00 add $5.00
$25.01 - $40.00 add $6.00
$40.01 - $50.00 add $7.00

$50.01 - $75.00 add $8.00
Over $75.00 add 9%

NAME
_____

CHURCH NAME
_____

ADDRESS
_____

CITY   STATE
_____

ZIP   PHONE
_____

E-MAIL

○ VISA ○ MASTERCARD   Make checks payable to: Christ Life Publications

_____
Card#   EXPIRATION DATE

_____
SIGNATURE REQUIRED

Christ *Life*
PUBLICATIONS
P.O. Box 399
Vinton, VA 24179

Website: **www.christlifemin.org**
E-mail: **info@christlifemin.org**
Phone: **(540) 890-6100**
Fax: **(540) 890-4133**